Praise for *Dancing About Architecture*

I remember saying a few years ago that in order for education to become relevant to our students, we would need to work hard to turn it into the new rock 'n' roll! Well, Phil Beadle may well be the lead guitarist of this new super group. Here is a book about teaching, and more importantly, learning, that is cool, irreverent and entertaining! From the reference to Frank Zappa in Chapter One, I knew this book was pure Phil Beadle. Buy it, read it and get ready to rock out!

Richard Gerver
Educational commentator, author and broadcaster

Phil Beadle's new book, *Dancing About Architecture*, is a well thought through testament to the power of creativity and the arts in education. Drawing on artists' thinking across disciplines, Phil explores how connecting seemingly disparate ideas results in work that can astound, inform and surprise. He encourages the educator to focus on process, not outcome, in much the same way that an artist focuses on process. This inevitably means taking risks – if the process becomes the focus, then risk taking becomes something joyful and, ironically, risk free – what does it matter if tangents happen when the outcome is not primary or set in stone?

Any educator that tries out the very practical and applicable ideas and resources in this accessible, and concise book will find themselves part of a journey of discovery with their students; they'll become a part of the process in a different, more immediate way; and even more pertinently, they'll get to experience the joy of creative thinking and practice and the endless possibilities it throws up. Phil respects and acknowledges the teacher as an intelligent, talented, creative individual and offers them the possibility of reclaiming the classroom as a place of possibility, more effective learning and exploration, free of the anxiety of the Ofsted inspection, that most bogus of pantomimes.

The kind of practice outlined in *Dancing About Architecture* means the whole student is engaged, mind and body. This is learning they'll retain because it engages all of them in unexpected and playful ways. The rigid hierarchy of what subjects 'matter' and the sheer aridity of sit-behind-a-desk-and-do-a-worksheet that's been set up by hundreds of years of academic hegemony is thrown into sharp relief as the nonsense that it is in this book. We were, as Phil points out, not evolved to sit behind a desk and do a worksheet. Personally, I can't think of anything more dreary.

The practice outlined in *Dancing About Architecture* is, ultimately, common sense. This book kicks the desks over, opens the windows and lets learning in – it invites us to live life in a more joyful, human way. You won't regret giving it a go. Equally, anyone who is interested in the possibilities of how their child can be educated or in creative thinking, and especially those in the arts – and especially those who happen teach in the arts, whether that's in a school or like myself, in an arts setting –

should give this a read. I've learnt a thing or two, and I've been working and teaching in the arts all of my adult life. In short, I highly recommend this book – it's a guide to the bright future of education.

Mhairi Grealis
Course Director, The Richmond Theatre
Creative Learning Co-ordinator, Music4children

Phil Beadle has not only written an excellent book ... he has designed a masterpiece for creativity-led education. Let this be your bible of learning theory and practice. I predict Beadle's next book will be a collection of examples from people like you – teachers, parents, policy makers, change managers, innovation specialists, volunteers – about how the ideas and practical tools in *Dancing About Architecture* have transformed your thinking about education, producing results worth shouting and writing about. Don't miss Beadle's invitation to dance ... your fitness in all matters educational is guaranteed to improve towards athletic proportions. Don't ignore this building block for the future of education. It contains the blueprint for architecting hours of fun in the classroom as well as serious learning results. Where Sir Ken Robinson tells us what to do in education, Beadle show us how to do it.

Kwela Sabine Hermanns, Innovation Specialist

My expectations for this book were very high from the moment I received it. As part of the Independent Thinking Series and with the now infamous Phil Beadle as the author the pressure that such a small book was under was quite immense.

I finished the book within a couple of hours and to be honest couldn't wait to get rid of it. Why? Simple really; the power of this book to transform the practise and views of my teaching staff is potentially huge. Phil has written a book that is accessible to all, compelling in its arguments, provocative in its thoughts and, best of all, heavily supported with practical examples and ready to go resources. In short, this book opens a universe of possibility, threading creativity through the very fabric of life and ultimately making learning fun and memorable. And it made me laugh. Not bad for a book that fits in your pocket!

**Paul Bannister, Headteacher,
Asfordby Captains Close Primary School**

The David Byrne – or is that Stan Bowles of Pedagogy?

Bracing pedagogical frolics with a sharp intellectual underpinning.

**Ian Whitwham, SecEd columnist,
journalist and former teacher**

... if he could convince Ofsted to accept even some of his methods, that would indeed be a step in the right direction! I believe that this is a book which should be available in every staff-room. Whether every teacher should have one – I'm not so sure ...!

Derek Henderson, Retired Primary Principal

I thought the book was both an interesting and thought provoking read. It was humorous and very truthful about teaching 'in the real world with real kids'. I especially enjoyed the chapter entitled 'the classroom as a stage' as it forced me to re-evaluate my drama lessons and I feel, after reading this specific chapter, that not only have my lessons improved, but I feel more confident in teaching using a different format.

As a teacher who likes to pride herself on her creativeness, I also found the 'resource' section of the book useful and have tried and tested many of the sport related ideas and it has definitely awoken a new passion for linking English to sport! Additionally, I have found that using the 'Rock and Roll' suggestions has mixed up my lessons more and resulted in both myself and (more importantly) my pupils being less bored by the same old boring routine us teachers often find ourselves stuck into. So much so I know keep a copy in my desk for when boredom of both the pupils and myself threatens to strike!

After reading it, I am now inspired to be more innovative while teaching and have more courage to just go with the flow/any random idea that pops into my head and I have seen evidence that this has drastically improved my lessons. I look forward to reading any other books Beadle has written and to, like him, finding an idea to use cut out footsteps for ... I feel some kind of punctuation tango may be in order ...

**Bridget Tolliday, English Teacher,
Rossett School, Harrogate**

Now, we should all get this – the power of creativity and the importance of arts in education. I certainly do because I worked on the now defunct Creative Partnerships programme. In my experience of encouraging teachers to rediscover their innate creativity, some jumped on board with gusto while others thought the programme was too messy, too noisy, too disruptive and too risky.

Mr Beadle of course has been practising creative teaching techniques since he decided he had better get a proper job as a teacher rather than following the rock star route.

I happen to know that some teachers find the notion of creative teaching and learning pretty insulting partly because teaching is a creative occupation.

The trouble is it is increasingly difficult to make it so, what with the current governmental obsession with facts and discipline.

In this neat little tome, *Dancing About Architecture*, Mr Beadle eloquently and enthusiastically argues the importance of how bringing the arts into 'traditional' curriculum subjects will give students a deeper, more memorable and more meaningful learning experience. This means having a go at juxtaposing subjects, for example the well-known system of learning punctuation through kung fu moves.

To help, the author offers simple techniques and resources to help, including how to write poems based on mathematic principles, as well as mixing sport into all areas of the curriculum.

This is a great book to have at your fingertips to liven up a dull lesson. I'm sure readers of *Ink Pellet* 'get' Mr Beadle's approach.

It's just the rest of them. Isn't it?

Ink Pellet – **The Arts Magazine for Teachers**

Phil Beadle's inimitable style will be familiar to many and his passion for learning and desire to stir things up comes flooding through this small and very well-formed volume. His editor, Ian Gilbert, sets the tone when he opens the foreword thus: 'Creativity is like pornography. It's hard to define but you know what it is when you see it. And it can get you into a lot of trouble bringing it in to school.'

The book consists of a series of chapters that are designed to provoke and on the whole he succeeds in startling, getting the reader to laugh, to think and to re-think. His premise is that we have unused potential both in our curriculum and in our classrooms and he wants to shake us out of our torpor. He also offers a range of techniques for 'treating the arts as forms for pedagogy' rather than the arts being the (stultifying) content focus of tired pedagogical approaches. Rather than trying to liven up lessons with 'fun' starters, Beadle offers the prospect of the whole lesson being exciting, engaging and loaded with relevant content, surely the Holy Grail of teaching and learning?

Dancing About Architecture is a genuine proposition, as is the 'punctuation ballet' and the potential for a mashup of physics and rugby. The ideas presented in this book are achievable by beginning and experienced teachers, provided they have the desire to have fun themselves. The comic tone should not deceive the reader: this is a serious book which offers teachers the opportunity not to be bored or boring.

Elaine Hall, *Learning & Teaching Update*

DANCING ABOUT ARCHITECTURE

A Little Book of Creativity

Phil Beadle Edited by Ian Gilbert

Crown House Publishing Limited
www.crownhouse.co.uk - www.crownhousepublishing.com

First published by

Crown House Publishing Ltd
Crown Buildings, Bancyfelin, Carmarthen, Wales, SA33 5ND, UK
www.crownhouse.co.uk

and

Crown House Publishing Company LLC
6 Trowbridge Drive, Suite 5, Bethel, CT 06801, USA
www.crownhousepublishing.com

First published 2011. Reprinted 2012.

British Library Cataloguing-in-Publication Data
A catalogue entry for this book is available
from the British Library.

Print ISBN 978-184590725-9
Mobi ISBN 978-184590746-4
ePub ISBN 978-184590747-1

LCCN 2011925283

Printed and bound in the UK by
Gomer Press, Llandysul, Ceredigion

This book is dedicated to my wife,
Jennifer Eirlys Marie Owens

Foreword

Creativity is like pornography. It's hard to define but you know what it is when you see it. And it can get you into a lot of trouble bringing it into school. Like mobile phones.

Speak to many people, so-called experts, and read their books on creativity and you have the idea that the creative process is a world of rainbows, visualisation and tantric breathing. If the mention of the phrase 'creativity in the classroom' has you reaching for the sugar paper and Berols then you are missing a trick. It's not that you're wrong. You can be highly creative with a paper and pens. Look at Rolf Harris (who I have said elsewhere is a multiply-intelligent god amongst men). But there is a rougher, edgier, more controversial, more two fingers in-your-face, stick-it-to-the-man creativity that sometimes sits uneasily in our middle-class, middle England teacher-training world. And I've taught creativity to lifers in a maximum security prison so I feel I have a little authority here.

'Every act of creation,' Picasso said, 'starts with an act of destruction.'

Creativity means you have to make a bit of a mess. What, then, might you have to break to move things forward creatively in your classroom? In your school? In your life? If creativity is about breaking the rules (which is different from having no rules. Very different) what is it that you have to rip up and start again to make things better?

Even if it is working fine currently? And are you prepared to do it? 'We'd get into trouble for a starting a revolution!' as one lady told me at a school a while back. That's the trouble with revolutions. They mess with your diary.

And are you equipped to do it? As you already know, our state education system was designed to get people *not* to think for themselves. Four 'Rs', not three. Reading , writing, 'rithmatic and respect for those above you. Teachers, social betters, bosses, generals, royalty, God. They will let you know what to think, should it ever be required. That's what the *Daily Mail* is for.

Picasso doesn't tell you how to be creative though. Just how it starts. Breaking the rules doesn't guarantee creativity. It's just a prerequisite. If that's the case, where do those darned elusive ideas come from? Just how do you get old ideas out and new ones in.

Well, according to Dee Hock, the man behind the world's first trillion-dollar company, VISA, the starting point isn't so much about learning but about forgetting.

'Clean out a corner of your mind and creativity will instantly fill it.'

Nature abhors a vacuum and the same applies in your head. The trouble is, if there's nothing to replace the gap left behind when you clear out all your old rubbish then some new rubbish will come along to fill it. Like ITV 2. So, where do the new ideas come from to fill the void left by eliminating your old ones? This question of the derivation of ideas was one that was approached by an advertising man called James Webb Young in 1939. His short book, *A Technique for Producing Ideas,* became the seminal book on how to get ideas, good ones, into your head. (And having also been an advertising copywriter I understand his compunction.) Webb Young suggests the following five-step plan to generating great ideas:

Step One – Gather the raw material

Step Two – Digest the material

Step Three – Don't think

Step Four – Wait for the 'Ah ha!' moment to appear (and be ready when it does. Keep a notebook by your bed)

Step Five – Expose your idea to the light of day and see if it stands up to the glare

Part of the first step that we often overlook, however, is the need to feed our brains with all sorts of 'raw material' and not just the sort most related to our work. If all you do, as an educator, is read education books then you will never be very creative. You will never succeed in doing what Steve Jobs, the creative genius behind Apple (amongst other things), calls making a 'dent in the universe'. Genuine creativity needs a collision of ideas, something that will never happen if all your thoughts travel in the same direction. Arthur Koestler in his seminal book on creativity, *The Act of Creation*, talks about 'bisociation'. An idea travels in one direction and then suddenly is broadsided by another travelling in a different one. It is used in humour all the time. What's blue and white and climbs trees? A fridge in a denim jacket. That sort of thing.

Interestingly it is step three, though, where we most often fail in the search for new ideas - the 'do nothing' part. Thinking hard is often – usually – the worst possible to way to think creatively about anything. Not thinking is one of the greatest thinking tools you can share with young people. Another advertising great, David Ogilvy, used to suggest that during this incubation stage the best thing to do was to take a bath, a stroll or a bottle of claret. 'The better the claret, the better the ideas,' he once said.

When I was in advertising, once I had read the papers or whatever it was I was feeding my mind with, I would sit with my feet up staring into space. However, for the 'suits' whose job it was to sell my creativity (and claim it as their own) this was always greeted with a great deal of derision. I imagine it would be the same for you. If someone came into your office or classroom whist you were sitting with your eyes closed, feet up and Classic FM on the radio what would be your reaction? Exactly. But would they prefer you did your job without thinking ... ?

Being creative is often about breaking taboos, challenging those around you, deliberately going a different route. Richard Branson credits his dyslexia for his penchant for creativity. His mind couldn't get 'from A to B' at school like his peers he once said, so he had to find creative ways to succeed, diversions around the mental roadblock. Whether by necessity or by choice creativity means doing things differently. 'Do things no one does or do things everyone does in a way no one does' as we like to refer to it in Independent Thinking. Which brings us to the controversial Mr Beadle.

While you might not like beige you don't actually notice it and any distaste for it is not worth breaking into a sweat over. Phil is like that, but the opposite. He fought his way up to overnight stardom in the working-class schools of East London, both as a student and as a teacher. Creativity and survival go hand in hand there. But that's just it. Phil isn't creative to make the world a nicer place. He's creative because sometimes the world sucks and you need to give it a kick to make it suck less. He won a *Teacher of the Year* award and made inflatable animals as part of his acceptance speech (and I was there to witness Eamonn Holmes' face stop being beige for a while). He won a Royal Television Society Award for his role in a controversial television programme that had him getting young people to read Shakespeare to cows and perform kung-fu to learn punctuation. He headed up another programme to teach adult non-readers how to read and had the nation weeping into their supper. He has his own regular column in *The Guardian*, a heady mix of wisdom and vitriol where NLP is akin to 'dog shit' and Michael Gove, the former minister of education (I'm planning ahead), is like Noddy. And many people hate him for it (do a search for his name in the 'online forum' section of the *Times Educational Supplement* website if you don't believe me). And it's not that he doesn't care. It's because he does. Passionately. Creatively. But his brand of creativity is not about sugar paper and Berols. It's about taking the world and giving it a kick. Before it kicks you. Again.

In this little book, Phil's first for the *Independent Thinking Series,* you will find many, many creative ideas to cut out and keep for your classroom or staff training session. Some ideas are quite straightforward. Some need the leap of faith that by asking different questions you will get different answers. Not always better but genuinely not what you expected. But giving you ideas is only part of what Phil – and the rest of Independent Thinking – is about. The name is the clue. What is more important is that you start to come up with your own ideas. This is where this little book can really help you. Yes, some of your ideas might fail. Live with it. Creativity and failure are bedfellows, Look at Jonathan Ross. On the other hand, they might succeed. Catastrophically, to borrow a phrase from the White House. Whatever happens, your world will start on that journey to upside down and you can screech to a halt in your grave with the universe well and truly battered.

Ian Gilbert, May 2011, Santiago
www.independentthinking.co.uk

Contents

Introduction

Steve Albini

If you do things the same way as everyone else, you'll get the same results as everyone else. Stands to reason. By definition, therefore, you will be average and the results you get will be average.

Let's have a look at average. He's a comfortable enough next-door neighbour alright, but you wouldn't want him coming to your house too often. Average doesn't get you drunk; it doesn't make you laugh, doesn't make you envious. In fact, average doesn't really do much, except borrow your lawnmower and bring it back not even properly broken. Average fails to satisfy.

No one spends their childhood dreaming of average. Few indeed are the children who have spent years lost in reverie at the ages of eight or nine thinking, 'One day, maybe one day, if I try to do everything I am told, if I follow the way that has been laid down for me by others, I will be the recipient of an award for conclusive mediocrity.'

The late advertising creative Paul Arden once said, 'You cannot produce great work by normal means. If you could everyone would be producing great work.' This is a

---

[1]   Steve Albini interview with lunakafe at www.lunakafe.com/moon73/usil73.php

1

shocking truth once you realise the veracity of it. It suggests that you must break the rules.

And you must. Not just because you are too lazy to follow them (though this sometimes creates an imperative). You must break the rules as a matter of policy – all day, every day, with a degree of rigour and dedication to the cause. The reason you must break the rules is that not breaking them is professionally negligent. Following the rules leads to being probably just about as good as everyone else and therefore perpetuates the cause of average. Copying a bunch of idiots eventually makes you an idiot: a moronic cut-out from a mediocre comic. Confounding the expectations that are set for you is entirely the best means possible of maintaining your personal and professional integrity.

The people you work for (and I mean the children you teach, not the bloke in the flash suit telling you that you're not good enough at your job) deserve better than working alongside a sheep-like copy of every unquestioned bad idea they've ever encountered. They desire and deserve you to be brilliant. You do not get to be brilliant by doing it the same way as everybody else does.

So.

Rip it up.

And start again.[2]

---

[2] Edwyn Collins and Orange Juice, *Rip it Up*

Juxtaposition

When things are novel, they are probably things we have discovered by accident or investigation rather than by design.[3]

Steve Albini (again)

Draw an operating table in the space I have left for you between this paragraph and the next. It doesn't have to be good or anything.

---

[3]   Steve Albini Op Cit

Well done for doing the picture. It was for practice. You are going to have to draw another one (fail better this time).[4] But there is a difference. Now, and it is crucial that it is a chance meeting (they didn't ring each other up and arrange to meet – it's an accident), draw the chance meeting of an umbrella and a sewing machine on top of a dissecting table.

---

[4] 'Ever tried. Ever failed. No matter. Try Again. Fail again. Fail better,' Samuel Beckett, *Worstward Ho* (1983). You know this though. Don't you?

Well done. Perhaps your drawing looked something like this?

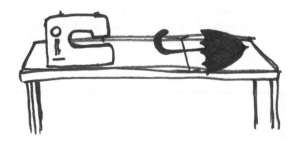

Now, I'm afraid, you must do some writing. I want you to write fifty words (forty-nine or fifty-one will not do at all). Those fifty words must be an analysis of the picture you have drawn, and that analysis must be from a specific perspective. You will argue that:

EITHER – the drawing is obsessed with death (a nihilistic interpretation if you will),

OR – it is obsessed with sex (Freudian perhaps)?

Do it here.

Here are a few examples of the work of some of the talented teachers who, in the past, I've asked to perform the same task:

Obviously, one cannot help but view M. Mulchrone's work without seeing the transparent references to sex – the silken texture of the umbrella as a phallus edging ever closer to the hard, unwieldy machine. The circular surface closest to the umbrella mimics most cleverly the female genitalia, as we can clearly see.

It was a large table. The umbrella fluttered as the sewing machine vibrated. Its cogs turn, getting closer and louder. The umbrella opened up all a quiver, flapping away. The vibrations the sewing machine caught in its open material. Was this the same machine that had stitched it up before?

How can I compare thee to an operation? I have just come on a summer breeze and there you stand, elegant, waiting, until I turn you on. You fill me with thread.

(This is not fifty words. See me.)

Clearly, these teachers are no strangers to perverse practice(s). Crucially, though, they've managed to keep it hidden. (This, I believe, goes by the name of professionalism.) However, if I had stood before them (or you) on a wet Tuesday morning and asked them (or you) to write me some soft-core eroticism, how might they have responded? Might they have refused? Would some have been so demotivated by the task that they could not go so far as putting pen to paper? Had I just jumped straight in and asked you to write some surreal eroticism without the aid of the visual stimulus, would you have done it?

So, teacher, what do we learn?

That there is, and must always be, more than one way to get to the outcome you want. That clever planning, structuring and scaffolding can deliver an outcome that, if shared at the start, would be greeted with resistance. Perhaps, we also learn that sometimes the outcome should not be defined at all. If we define the outcome we get what we expect. Getting what we expect often comes with accompanying disappointment. 'Great,' we gurn, 'They did exactly what I wanted them to do.' Ho hum. No alarms, then. No surprises. It all turned out as planned.

However, if we are prepared to experiment, to focus on process and let 'outcome' float around on the breeze waiting to be discovered, something different happens. We either fall flat on our behinds, or we discover new lands; and you cannot discover new lands by keeping one foot in the old country. So jump, happily, knowing that the process of learning to be brilliant involves risk. As a teacher, it is always worth taking a risk. Your audience will forgive you if it doesn't work. They will also feel the thrill of the high wire along with you when you walk it.

What else do we learn from the exercise? We learn that juxtaposition helps us see things in completely new ways.

The idea of something being as 'beautiful as the chance meeting on a dissecting table of a sewing machine and an umbrella' was coined by Comte de Lautréamont, the writer of *Les Chants de Maldoror*. The phrase was taken up by André Breton and became a definition of a new art movement: Surrealism. The 'beauty' of which Lautréamont spoke is caused by taking things that do not ordinarily go together and juxtaposing them – placing them side by side, and seeing what happens.

Here is a picture of a man. Shall we call him David? What are the first three things you notice about him?

Now he is standing next to someone else. What similarities or differences do you note?

We see more of the detail in David when we stand him next to someone else. This is one way in which juxtaposition works. It brings new light to things we might otherwise have made assumptions about. Having a further object to contrast it with allows us to see how it is different to that object. It may also help us to see things they share. Either way we see new things.

And it is good to see new things.

A phrase that suggests just such a version of seeing is 'dancing about architecture'. It is commonly (mis)attributed to Frank Zappa, as an accusation of uselessness on the part of people who write about music: 'Y'know, maaaan,' puff of insanely fat roll-up, tweak of goatee beard, 'writing about music, maaan,' further puff, 'is just about as useful as dancing about architecture.' Acolytes nod in agreement. No one questions imbecility of statement.

I think the (mis)attribution is probably the result of Zappa once saying: 'Rock journalism is people who can't write interviewing people who can't talk in order to provide articles for people who can't read.'[5] But we can't really pin the idea on the brother and so have variously (mis)attributed it to Elvis Costello, Brian Eno (more of whom later) and David Byrne. No one really knows from whose lips it first came, but it has spread as an idea.

Why?

Because, in opposition to the original intent of this juxtaposition (which was to highlight an absurdity) dancing about architecture is obviously, unquestionably and indubitably, the right thing to do. If we consider Gaudí's Sagrada Família in Barcelona, for instance, we might

---

5 Puff of obscenely fat roll-up, tweak of goatee beard, acolytes nod in agreement, no one questions imbecility of statement.

wonder about the most appropriate way to investigate it. In any sane world, surely, performing a dance about it *must* be one of the most sensible ways of going about such an investigation.

The idea of dancing about the Sagrada Família brings up the specific version of juxtaposition that is at the heart of this book. Sir Ken Robinson, whose name always comes with the accompanying epithet, 'an internationally recognised expert on creativity', defines creativity as, 'the process of having original ideas that have value'[6] and goes on to state that such creativity normally occurs, 'through the interaction of different disciplinary ways of seeing things'.[7]

We create the new not generally through some mad moment of inspiration in fictionalised accounts of ancient Greeks in baths (though the conditions for this can be forced into existence), but by putting things together that do not normally go together; from taking disciplines (or curriculum areas) and seeing what happens when they are forced into unanticipated collision.[8]

Sir Ken's chief influence in this statement is, I believe, an advertising executive from the post-war years, James Webb Young, who once described himself as being someone 'who has had to earn his living by producing what were *alleged* to be ideas'.[9]

---

[6] Sir Ken Robinson, www.ted.com/
[7] Ibid.
[8] Everything is linked, but not everyone sees it.
[9] James Webb Young, *A Technique for Producing Ideas*, new edn (New York: McGraw-Hill Professional, 2003).

Webb Young's *A Technique for Producing Ideas* suggests that to create a new idea of value you merely take two disciplines that do not appear to belong together and force them through a blender, because 'an idea is nothing more nor less than a new combination of old elements',[10] and that a person with a propensity to produce ideas will be someone who sees the relationship between things; relationships that are not necessarily obvious on first sight.

The mind, at its best, is a pattern-making machine, engaged in a perpetual attempt to impose order on to chaos; making links between disparate entities or ideas in order to better understand either or both. It is the ability to spot the potential in the product of connecting things that don't ordinarily go together that marks out the person (or teacher) who is truly creative.

For evidence of how this might be confirmed as historical truth you need look only as far as the history of non-classical music. Genres cross-pollinate; accidentally producing new flowers. Cross the blues with skiffle and you've got Elvis; further cross the blues with gospel and, baby, you got soul; mash up electro with rap, *eh voila* le hip hop. All major developments in musical genre have come from this process.

One of Sir Ken's most seductive ideas is his identification of the most ridiculous facet of the British, or indeed any, education system: the fact that it tends to ignore the existence of the nine-tenths of the child below the neck.

---

[10] Webb Young, *A Technique for Producing Ideas*, p. 15.

We are not pure intellect in spirit form. As a species, it is possible we may one day evolve out of our bodies, but it is unlikely to be this academic year. We should not, I think, be banning children from using their bodies in a place of learning. Letting them know that their bodies are not important to how they learn is, I think, a lesson of negative value.

How then to ensure that we respect our students' physicality, their very being?

There is a solution.

If we combined the head (academic subjects) with the body (arts-based subjects), would this be a synthesis that leads to interesting learning experiences for our students? Let's examine this a while. What happens when we treat the arts as forms of pedagogy themselves?

If we take Webb Young's theory and try it out by writing ten things we might want to teach in an English lesson on one piece of paper, and a further series of ten disciplines or artistic sub-genres on another, cut these up and then pair them up entirely randomly, what do we get? The adverbial tap dance; a conjunctions melodrama; the surrealist painting of an apostrophe (or the surrealist apostrophe, painting); funk paragraphing; the exclamation mark ballet! The genius of course would be in the implementation, but certainly a committed practitioner with a class of children who trust their teacher would be able to produce lessons generated by this process far removed from the humdrum educational world of photocopied worksheet and the barely stifled yawn.

It suggests to me the first infinitesimal chink of light to fall on a new world that might be forced into being. If we were to take the box currently marked 'cross-curricular links' as asking us an entirely different question to the one it currently presents – that new question being, 'How are you going to use the arts as pedagogical method in this lesson?' – what improvements might be made to the educational experience of the children we teach? Period 1: the quadratic equations ballet; period 2: remaking the Bayeux Tapestry for the Second World War; periods 3 and 4: double dancing about politics; period 5: science as seen through the prism of a Jimi Hendrix guitar solo. Would such lessons be anti-intellectual? Could you fit in all the course content required? Or would we have to design a whole new model to make it work?

The message that the arts, as disciplines, are underused can be used as a ground zero; a point from which we might extemporise. If the arts are wrongly placed as the spindly base of an inverted pyramid, at the top of which sit number and language, what would happen if we altered their position so that they had equal status? Furthermore, what would happen if we not only evened out that hierarchy but took the notion of disciplines colliding as being the path towards creating new things?

We might come up with something entirely new.

The arts in schools loosely divide into:

Music

Visual art

Drama

Sport

Dance

And are viewed as having exactly that hierarchy in terms of the value they are ascribed.

Music is not only very difficult, but it has a series of respected, dead European progenitors: Bach, Bartók, Beethoven and Brahms. It is also a branch of mathematics and must therefore be ascribed more status than dance, which is just responding to the maths.

Visual art also confers immortality on its most famous practitioners. It is an intrinsic part of what makes Europeans feel culturally superior to everyone else. It is ascribed value therefore.

Drama has a rich history, but is populated by humans who feel the need to perform and who are seen as an embarrassment by some.

Sport is the preferred pastime of the barely literate.

Dance, too, is for dunces; but unlike sport you cannot achieve iconic status through it or get paid for doing it, unless you are Russian or are prepared to spend your evenings scantily clad in a cage in a nightclub.

There is an odious academic convention: where academics present their research in book or article form they write what they call an 'introduction'. In it, they tell you what they are going to do.

When reading these things I always scream inwardly, 'Don't waste three pages and five minutes of my life telling me what you are going to do. Get on with it professor!' I have promised myself that I will never ever write so much as a paragraph that does such a job.

Over the body of this book I propose to look at ways that we might use the arts as forms of pedagogy and, more specifically, how one might use process-led collisions of art forms to produce new learning experiences for our students.[11]

---

[11] It's only a small paragraph.

Dancing about Architecture

The secret of dancing is that you must respect and admire your partner. Thus, entropy isn't the enemy, and the goal isn't for 'everything to be all right'. Without random events, there is no dance. There is no good, there is no bad, there's just what happened. Dance with it.

Seth Goodin[12]

Let's start from the bottom up. Perhaps as an acknowledgement of the unarguable vibrancy of some of the street forms of dance (though, more probably, because some petty bureaucrat rather enjoys sitting, gorging himself on chow mein whilst sweating in front of *Strictly Ballroom*), schools seem to have cottoned on to the fact that dance in the inner cities is an art form that forms a path away from seeking prestige in the gang. Like sport, it causes young people to work as a team. Unlike sport, they work to create something that is arguably not almost entirely ephemeral.

Soul brother number one, Mr James Brown, once argued, 'Ain't no problem in the world can't be cured by dancing.' This might be held as a guiding principle for the investigative teacher. He also said, 'Get on off of that thing'; a further manifesto from which the desk-bound might benefit.[13]

---

12 Seth Goodin, blog at http://sethgodin.typepad.com/
13 Another inspiring James Brown lyric is, 'I feel like a sex machine', which some might deem inappropriate in a primary school setting.

If you have ever had the chance to witness a group of inner-city kids immersed in a dazzling street-dance performance, you will have seen the living embodiment of James Brown's philosophical utterances. Dancing, for some, is a mainline to joy, a sensual ecstasy, a means of displaying mastery, a chance to escape from the drudgery of being behind a desk and a confirmation of the obvious truth that millions of years of evolution were not meant to land us cooped up in a classroom listening to someone older than us speak about something in which we have no interest. It also introduces an alternative version of masculinity to that of the hegemonic variety; one that comes with the chemical, physical rewards of mugging or running away from the police but, not only carries substantially less risk of imprisonment, also leads somewhere. If we want our young people to display more discipline we could do worse than introducing them to a few. Dancing to any level requires, and is a, discipline.

However, recent massive improvements in the standard and status of dance education have been limited to the dance department and, further, in a plausibly racist move, to those dance departments that serve communities with a large number of black people in them. What if all PGCEs had a two-day component so that all teachers were sufficiently trained in teaching the rudiments of dance? Would this transform kids' experiences of education for the worse or for the better? Furthermore, would the buttoned-down students at the country's elite places of learning (or places of *learning* the elite) benefit more from hurting each other playing rugby or from celebrating their physicality through dance?

How might we take dance out of the studio and into the classroom? Here's an idea. Rhythm applies in any area of the curriculum that employs either number or interval. Dance works like this too.

Let us look at punctuation. It separates down into periods and intervals.

The period:

. ? !

What do these three share? The notation at the bottom: a full stop. And what does this mark on a page indicate? That the reader must take a pause of the same length for each. And the marks above it for both the question and the exclamation? They are notation of intonation.

Punctuation is therefore a form of musical notation.

The interval confirms this:

, ; :

Why is literacy an issue? One reason might be that the vast majority of English teachers do not touch upon this notation, as they are scared of it and (many) do not have any mature understanding of how it works. (I recently had an involved conversation about the semicolon with an Oxford graduate, which resulted in both of us admitting that neither of us, after many years of fighting, were anywhere near taming the beast).

Might it be possible to create a ballet based upon these pieces of notation, and if so, what would the punctuation ballet look like?

By way of answer: in 1972, the American composer Steve Reich created a minimalist piece of two performers clapping; one holding down a 12/8 rhythm, the other holding down the same rhythm, but shifting the timing around so the sounds created by the two performers phased. Could we combine this with a series of specific moves to signify various punctuation marks? Could we further mix this up with a PowerPoint synchronised to fire off at various intervals pieces of information about usage? What would happen if we did?

If this were possible then could we take it further and dance more complex intervals or forms of notation? Could we dance algebra? What moves might accompany

$$3x = 4?[14]$$

Could we dance a whole series of square roots? Or perhaps we might dance trigonometry?

Sine =	$\dfrac{\text{opposite}}{\text{hypotenuse}}$	Difficult though not impossible.
Cosine =	$\dfrac{\text{adjacent}}{\text{hypotenuse}}$	Hard too.
Tangent =	$\dfrac{\text{opposite}}{\text{adjacent}}$	Entirely plausible.

---

[14] It is a half-hour well spent considering this conundrum with a piece of paper and a pencil to hand.

And if our white, male overbite made us too embarrassed to dance, how might we dance about algebra, punctuation or architecture without actually getting on up off that thing or acting like a sex machine?

An answer might be that we could draw the dance we would have done, had we not been educated into being too acutely embarrassed at the way we moved our bodies to be free with them. And, in doing so, we would go through a further process or stage of reconstituting or reprocessing the information coming up with another unexpected outcome.

Here is what a teacher at Thomas More School in Croydon produced when asked to draw a dance about the Sagrada Família.

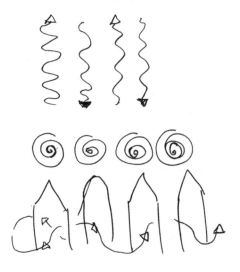

Cleverly, some deliberately leave the dance or drawing unfinished.

Through the process of taking one form and examining it through two others, she has created an entirely new, if abstract, means of notating dance. Now, if I had asked her to do so directly on a wet Tuesday morning, she may have scratched her head and sat with a blank piece of paper for a full month.

What fascinates here is the infinity of potential in having the outcome completely led by process. If we take Gardner's intelligences as being a guiding structure and run them back to front, the lesson outcome would be a thought: a thought about speech about an image of a piece of music, which is written about numbers that have been obtained from a literary text. As an example, if we take Edward Kamau Brathwaite's 'Limbo' (the numerical aspects of which are examined in the 'Speaking in Number' chapter) as a basis, we could take these num-bers, use them to create a piece of music which would be the stimulus for a drawn image that has been discussed at length, and about which students have individually drawn a conclusion after deep thought.

'But where are your lesson objectives?'

'I don't know, Mr Lesson Inspector. We were trying to grasp at things we couldn't possibly ever understand.'

Ask Your Body

I have a friend (I have few). At the age of forty-eight she travelled with two children, a knackered bag and no money, back to England far away from where she had lived in the Caribbean. You do not start a new life at nearly fifty. It is beyond the probable. This person did. Within ten years of returning to England, owning little more than the shoes she walked in, she had revolutionised the way that writing was taught in primary schools to such a degree that more or less every primary school in the country now teaches writing the Ros Wilson way. She is exceptionally good company in a bar and is a long way distanced from the ordinary.

Among the battery of genius ideas Ros has either originated or popularised is Kung Fu Punctuation.[15] If you have not encountered it, she ascribes a series of kung fu style moves and sounds to each punctuation mark. It is improbable. And utterly brilliant. It sets off ideas ...

If it is possible to teach those esoteric dots on a page through a martial art, a sport, how else might one use organised physical activity? What combinations might there be?

On the next two pages there is a list of subject areas and a further list of sports. Photocopy each page and then cut them up (alternatively find them at the rear of the book in the Resources section ready to be cut up). Devise a

---

[15] Though its correct attribution is to a teacher called Liz.

method to randomly match a sport to a subject area. Then decide how you might use the moves of that sport in lessons to illuminate the subject. Crucially, it is the moves. We do not teach history through wrestling by teaching the history of wrestling. What we are looking for, grapple fans, is something in the region of the class conflict arm wrestle, submission to equations, religion's two falls or one submission.

English – Reading	Snooker
English – Writing	Darts
English – S and L	Football
Maths	Netball
Statistics	Hockey
Physics	Rugby
Chemistry	Cricket
Biology	Sprinting

RE	Egg and Spoon
Geography	Hurdling
History	Wrestling
Sociology	Boxing
French	Tennis
ICT	Golf
Technology	Cycling
Citizenship	Disability Sport
PSHE	Swimming

Let's see what happens when we just put them in the order they are on the page already.

Discard what doesn't jump out at us and we are left with ideas.

☐ **French and tennis**. Tennis lends itself readily to educational activities, as it involves turn taking. More or less any speaking and listening activity can be easily adapted so that it takes on the form of a tennis match; adversarial, back and forth, involving constant repositioning. This could quite easily be done in another language: *un match de tennis conversationel*.

☐ **Speaking and listening and football**. The football pitch is a realm with a language all of its own: 'Terry's ball', 'heads up', 'face up', 'out', 'wide', 'switch', 'overlap'. All of these model the clarity of communicating sophisticed ideas (language as a sign) that the one-word or two-word interjection can convey. Furthermore, if you do not listen properly to your captain's call as he rises for a header, you may well have your head broken. Sit as a class and watch a football match for examples of verbal and non-verbal communication, record these, then bring it all back inside and see what we can take from football in terms of the way we communicate with each other. Are some of the more subtle forms of non-verbal communication useful in our grouped discussions? (For more on this see the obscure pamphlet *Literacy through Football Skills* by me.)[16]

☐ **Writing and darts**. Can we learn anything about how to improve our penmanship from a study of the grip of such athletic greats as Jocky Wilson or Bobby 'Dazzler' George? Would transcribing the speech of Sid Waddell be of educational benefit? He once

---

[16] Phil Beadle, *Literacy Through Football Skills* (Crown House 2009).

uttered the phrase, 'quintessential darts!' What does this mean? Is it correct usage? He also coined the phrase, 'Jocky at the ocky'. Any study of internal rhyme would benefit from starting here. His utterance, 'Jocky Wilson. What an athlete!' might finally give us the dictionary definition of irony that English teachers have longed for for such eons.

☐ **Maths and netball**. Angles. Does a pass at a thirty-degree angle go further or less far than one at forty-five degrees?

☐ **Physics and rugby**. Velocity, force and mass. What equation do we need to calculate for whether Shavonne can knock over Jordan?

☐ **Religious education and egg and spoon** is a pleasing combination, though it is difficult to locate which of the two elements might be the more valuable educationally. Now children, you can either believe that there is a man in the sky, who no one has ever seen, and who knows what you are thinking, or you can find value in transporting a hard-boiled egg from one place to another on a dessert spoon.

Try your own combinations. Alternatively, run the lesson you have to teach up against each of these sports and see what comes up. Maybe you can reach in the direction of the more obscure sport. How might we model usage of parentheses through pelota? (Pelota is a Basque ball game involving throwing a very hard ball at extremely high speeds towards a whimpering opponent.)

The Classroom As Stage

There is a theatrical style called bouffant clowning. Bouffants are grotesque and deformed: they have grossly exaggerated facial expressions and gestures. When I first started teaching bouffant clowning to fifteen-year-old drama students in Canning Town, east London, many of the students cried hurt tears of righteous anger. They felt it was too close to being an uninformed, clumsy and morally unconscionable satire of people with profound learning difficulties. I was proud of them and of their reaction.

I was also proud of having come up with a lesson that – entirely accidentally – caused them to show what they were made of. The defined outcome was that they would know the generic conventions of bouffant clowning; the real outcome was that they clarified their ideas as to what is and is not morally acceptable in a classroom. Which was the better outcome: the defined or the accidental?

If you want to know what can be achieved in a classroom go and see your school's best teacher of drama. Learn from them. Copy them. Pretend to be them. For in their classes you will see teaching without fear, without stock reliance on the desk, the pencil and the shout. Should every teacher in the country be drama trained?

Will they be?

Drama teachers work with things they call drama forms. Some (not all) of these are transferable to any curriculum area. It is worth knowing what they are though, and examining how you might use them in other areas. However, I will not be bothering to pad out this book with a description of hot seating or forum theatre, because hot seating is for dullards and forum theatre (in which the kids are allowed to stop the proceedings and suggest an alternative cause of action for the characters) is, like rock musicians at any point in their career discovering an interest in Indian mysticism[17], the province of the scoundrel.

Drama Forms

Thought-Tracking

'I like your shoes.' (*However, I note that they fail quite singularly in covering up your unforgiveable ankles.*)

'Thank you ever so much. Did I forget to congratulate you on your new boyfriend? He is très, très charmant.' (*If you have a taste for poly-drug-addicted, sexually profligate, jobless liars. And as if I would look for fashion tips from Coco the Clown! And will you stop looking at my ankles.*)

We don't always say what we mean. Most of time we just go through the socialised rigmarole of acceptable communicational norms. In short, we spend half our time

---

[17] I refer here specifically to the worst band of all time: Kula Shaker.

lying. What would happen if the truth of what we really thought was revealed? What if, rather than politely and half-embarrassedly intoning the none-more-repetitiously-hollow phrase of 'Good morning' to the colleagues to whom we are so utterly ambivalent, we replied, 'No. It isn't. If it were I would not be here. And I most certainly wouldn't be exchanging meaningless unpleasantries with you, sir, who are the very dictionary definition of specious'?

Thought-tracking is a drama form where these secret thoughts are voiced, generally by another performer who, it is likely, will be standing behind the performer who is mouthing the platitudes. It is usually performed in fours. Two performers have the ordinary conversation, and two voice their real thoughts. Like so:

A: Some of my best friends are black.

A's thought-tracker: (Not many though.)

B: Mine too.

B's thought-tracker: (Well there's Reg from school, who I haven't seen since 1984.)

A: I don't understand racism at all.

A's thought-tracker: (That Nick Griffin is a handsome and intelligent man.)

B: Me neither.

B's thought-tracker: (Though I find Nick Griffin's animal charisma and outgrown, skinhead machismo sexually arousing.)

31

Anything that forces kids to look at the duplicitous nature of most of our spoken communication is of value in itself. Uncovering truths is a (the) fundamental part of education. In reality, I have found that kids' responses to this technique are not hugely satisfying. It takes a degree of intellectual deftness, and perhaps even sophistication, to do this at all well, and most of the times I have used this technique with students, the results have been not dissimilar to this exchange:

A: Nice shoes.

A's thought tracker: (They look like they come from Poundland.)

B: I like your hair.

B's thought tracker: (It looks like you got it cut at the pound shop, innit?)

A: Nice, erm, wot we do now sir, innit?

But, then again, I have only very rarely been allowed to stand in front of classes of those bred for greatness. (And there was always a member of the school's senior management present to ensure there was no real risk of them ever being told the truth about anything.)

Where thought-tracking works well is when kids move; when they are not stuck, stock-still, mouthing stilted lines, but have jumped into the form with the whole of their being. This can be used for a variety of subjects, anything in which you want to reveal how social veneer works, or what people's secret motivations are for actions. It could be of use in looking at the motives of multinational corporations in geography, examining political lies in history, revealing the real truth of what children feel about important issues in citizenship.

Freeze-Frame / Frozen Picture / Tableau

Depending on what decade is your favourite, you'll have a different name for this. In the seventies we called it a 'tableau' – you may recall a cardboard box with a piece of coloured film at one end in which were stuck some cardboard historical characters enacting a battle, in which case you might even refer to it as a 'diorama'. In the nineties it became the more prosaic 'freeze-frame' and the noughties the even more clunky 'frozen picture'. We will stick with 'tableau' as, being a French word, it implies a degree of academic respectability that we don't deserve, but fancy all the same.

Le Tableau Naturalistique

This is a still moment caught in time. It works best with four students, though five is permissible. In it, the kids act as if they were unconsciously caught by a camera, the action frozen. Being naturalistic, it captures moments from some dramatic approximation of reality: the moment Mandela was released, the moment they went over the trenches in the First World War, a mother lamenting a dying child in the Ethiopian famine. Anything that would make an interesting tableau that illuminates the curriculum.

There are several tips to creating the perfect tableau or frozen picture.

1. *Staying still* – A 'frozen' picture, part of what defines it is that students involved in it should be, erm, frozen. This can escape them. Particularly their heads. Students may have their hands out in a perfectly frozen gesture, pointing portentously towards some imagined future, while their heads are all a-wobble. The way to ensure that they remain frozen, no matter what absurdly difficult balancing act the rest of their body has to perform, is by focusing their eyes on a fixed point somewhere in the room, and keeping their eyes on that point no matter what.

2. *Variety of spatial levels* – A tableau is better if everyone is not standing at exactly the same height: have some kneel, some crawl, none jump (it doesn't work – think about it). Chairs are of use here. Good for sitting on. Double good for standing on.

3. *Finding a centre of gravity* – The best tableaux in *le mode naturalistique* really do look as if people have been frozen in the middle of some desperately important activity. When they are done well, this can create substantial demands on students' powers of balance. Imagine a photo of a football match; if most of the players were actually frozen as they launched into a tackle or swerved around a defender they would fall over, as they are only balanced in movement. It is worth taking students through the process of locating where your centre of gravity is when you have your foot raised. Again, focusing on a still point on the wall aids here.

Le Tableau Symbolique

These are the same as the naturalistic version, only not anywhere near being as naturalistic. They examine notions of status and relationships spatially.

What is the relationship here?

How has that relationship changed now?

What is happening now?

Who loves who?

Is it reciprocated? Alternatively, what do you think kneeling guy did wrong? Will he be forgiven, do you think?

We can tell an interesting and emotionally complex story merely by altering the spatial relationship between two entirely neutral characters. But the symbolic frozen picture can be taken much further than this. Human bodies do not necessarily have to represent human bodies caught in time. They can instead be taken, in freeze-frame, to represent ideas, concepts, themes or even a specific analysis of a text or historical event. I have spent many years attempting to understand this, from Act 4, Scene 1 of *Macbeth*:

A show of Eight Kings, the last with a glass in his hand; GHOST OF BANQUO following.[18]

---

[18] William Shakespeare, *Macbeth* (this stage direction is in every single edition I've read).

I am somewhere near understanding its significance. It has taken over thirty years, but I think this year will be the year I completely crack the code of what is basically a symbolic tableau.

It is difficult to set a single reader a piece of work that involves performing a physical activity with three other people so, unless you have ready access to three generous people with no sense of shame at all, draw the symbolic tableau you might have done in groups of four that could have illustrated the following:

The fact that the 'theory' of
learning styles is hogwash.

Images in poems are created by the poet's choice of which common nouns they use.

A squared + B squared = C squared.

Drawing the tableau does not come with the benefits of indulging in the satisfying horseplay of the physical; we are probably also less likely to remember it if we only draw what we might have done, but it has the same level of cognitive complexity in that it involves transforming the concrete to the abstract. Also, it has the same process-led, reprocessing effect we saw previously when we were drawing about dancing about architecture. (This time we're drawing about acting about maths.) It is when we process and reprocess knowledge through a variety of art forms that not only do we get interesting outcomes, but that knowledge tends to be understood more acutely, in greater depth and in more readily retainable form. And if the last stage of that reprocessing is a form of visual recording, we get the added benefit of some intriguing display work.

Snapshots

Here we use a series of five or so tableaux in sequence to create a narrative. Imagine the following.

Picture 1: two boxers sit on their chairs in their respective corners, both have their gloves at a 120-degree angle as their respective wrists are held by their trainers whose mouths are caught frozen in a moment of impassioned exhortation.

Picture 2: the fighters meet in the middle of the ring, towels around their necks, they eyeball each other.

Picture 3: the tableau catches the very moment that they touch gloves; a brief millisecond of comradeship before they tear into each other for the entertainment of a bloodthirsty crowd.

Picture 4: the challenger's fist is captured at the arc of the follow-through of a huge haymaker that fails to land; the favourite's upper torso sways backwards to avoid the punch.

Picture 5: the champ counters, the tableau frozen at the exact moment a bone-crunching thud lands squarely on the weak chin of the challenger.

Picture 6: the champ is still, in exultation, as he towers above the prostrate challenger. The trainers begin their climb through the ropes.

Snapshots can be used to dramatise, to see the inside of, to bring to life, anything to which a narrative can be attached. The technique can also be used on a more symbolic level for any process that goes through a series of stages. It could be used to exemplify, for instance, the various stages of thought a student might have to go through to perform a quadratic equation; or, somehow, students might use their bodies symbolically to show the various stages in the formation of an oxbow lake. Think about this. Would a geography lesson featuring snapshots to show how a physical process works be less or more interesting than reading a textbook about it, which features generic illustrations from the fifties?

There is a technical aspect to performing a series of snapshots that you would be wise to educate your kids in should you wish to use it. The secret is that the transitions must appear seamless. They must hold each tableau for a set period of time (say ten seconds) and then, maintaining utter neutrality during the transition, go from one picture to the next without fuss or any apparent communication. What they must not do is appoint someone in the group to say the word 'change' out loud, as this destroys both spectacle and illusion. What the group have to do is work out a means of signalling to each other that it is time to change from one picture to the other, without this being apparent to the audience. This might be that they all silently count up to a certain number in their heads, though there are issues here in that not all members of the group have exactly the same conception of time! Better is to appoint a group leader, a 'transition signaller', to do the counting individually and then to give an agreed signal to the rest of the group that is evident to them but imperceptible to the audience – the twitch of an index finger works well here. Though this sets up another dictate: that all group members must be frozen in a position from which they can clearly view that particular finger.

Another key here is that kids have to be taught the skills of neutrality: arms flat to their sides, focus only on the point to which they are travelling, a personality-free walk and face undefined by expression. The better they achieve neutrality during transitions, the more pronounced will be the drama when they go into the next tableau.

Again, if we want a recorded outcome here, this can either be achieved with the use of video cameras; with coloured pencils and a grouped or individual storyboarding activity; or with a pen, a blank sheet of A4 and a fertile mind.

Thoughts Aloud

This, at the whim of the teacher, is a device where we reveal, again, the real thoughts of a character during either an improvisation or a scripted piece. At any point of their choosing, the teacher shouts the word 'freeze' and the students do so. The teacher then calls the name of a student or the character they are playing and suffixes this with the instruction 'thoughts aloud'. The student then voices the exact thoughts of the character.

Voices of Conscience

Often Tom – on finding that Jerry was, at long, long last prostrate and begging for his pussycat stage partner not to eat him – would find his conscience pricking him. In Cartoonland the conscience was portrayed by having a mini-devil and mini-angel on either one of Tom's shoulders. 'Show mercy,' the petite angel would say (like the simpering wimp he is). 'Eat the f****ing mouse,' replied the devil cat, speaking to Tom's bad self – to what he really wanted. In the end, Jerry generally got away because poor old Tom had spent too much time thinking and not enough doing. That's the trouble with a conscience. It's always around when you least need it, and it'll stop you doing things you want to.

But, for those of you who want to instil a conscience as a worthwhile thing for kids to cultivate, then the drama form voices of conscience is a useful tool for examining the duality of their own desires, and those of any fictional or historic characters they might be studying. Basically, you re-enact the Tom and Jerry scene. It usually employs two different people circling a third who is sitting on a chair. When one of the characters in a book they are studying has a crisis of conscience, when they are studying the slave trade in history or the decisions a farmer has to make in geography, then voices of conscience is a decent tool to reveal the mind's inner workings.

Kids work in threes.[19] One plays the character with the crisis of conscience, the other two play either side of the argument. The angel and devil alternate giving advice, beseeching or entreating, while the character sits mute contemplating the alternating arguments. At the end of the display we discuss with the character which of the two arguments they felt was the more forceful.

Technically, this can result in a rather stilted piece of drama, in which there is little movement. The best results occur when the central character is standing and the voices of conscience circle round them like harpies, perhaps even having a tug of war with the character's arms; the character leaning bodily towards whoever they feel is winning the argument.

Thoughts Aloud into Sound
Collage or Monologue

First, you push the desks aside, leaving the entire classroom as a performance space. From thence, you arrange the chairs so that kids are seated, entirely individually, in as much space as you can muster. This particular version of classroom organisation is massively useful, in that it allows the kids' sole focus point to be their thoughts. There are few distractions, so that when a teacher offers the lone, all too rarely ever heard in British classrooms,

---

[19] There is an optional preparatory stage in which the kids, in threes, take a piece of paper, divide it two (a fold along the vertical axis is the quickest way of doing this), then write the reasons for a decision on one side, the reasons against it on the other. It informs their performance.

instruction 'Think about ... ', kids are able to do so at some length. We may have examined some stimulus material and then decided to spend one or two minutes just thinking about the things that material has brought up for them.

We may then call their names and ask them to offer their 'thoughts aloud' for the rest of the class. We might ask them to boil their thoughts into one word. From here we can perform a sound collage.

A sound collage is a collection of words that build up to create an aural slab or mass (or mess or wordle). You can perform it in many ways. Let's take the idea that the kids have been given some stimulus of an upsetting situation; they are asked to put themselves into the role of a character, to imagine themselves in their plight, to think for two minutes in role, then to boil down their emotion into one word. The teacher either asks for their word on the count of three, which leads to a brief, cataclysmic, though ultimately unsatisfactory, wail.

A better way of doing it is asking kids to say their word, out loud, three times at the moment the teacher passes them. The teacher starts at one end of the room, arms splayed out like wings, and slowly walks from one side of the room to the other. After a brief rehearsal, this works very well, and we receive, for our efforts, a collage which gives us access to the feelings of the character we are examining, be they of the dramatic variety or some real-life figure with whom we might want to try to empathise. How did Blair feel on sending soldiers to their death in an illegal war? Can we have sympathy for a war criminal?

Another way of using this set-up and start is, rather than reducing the volume of words, adding to them. Taking their thoughts aloud, we ask them to build them into one sentence, then into two; then we ask them to take the great leap of faith into a full monologue.

I spoke at a conference a couple of years ago immediately prior to an educator by the name of Sir Dexter Hutt. We are probably not of the type who would normally gravitate towards each other, as I think if I worked for him he would probably sack me pretty quickly. (This becomes apparent almost immediately whenever I find myself accidentally working alongside a knighted head teacher.) However, he said something about the curriculum and its suitability for preparing kids for the modern world that struck a chord: much of the modern working world involves and requires skills in presenting to an audience, big or small, and we devote neither time, status nor any particularly skilled professional expertise to teaching kids how to do this. Giving kids time to practise performing monologues in front of each other would give them the opportunities to make their mistakes and learn how to overcome the crushing fear of the stage in a more forgiving environment than they would receive if their first ever presentation was for high stakes in some old boardroom or other.

Pretty Ugly Things

To some extent I happily don't know what I'm doing. I feel that it's an artist's responsibility to trust that.[20]

David Byrne

Visual art is both stimulus and method of recording. Teachers are good, I think, at the former. It is not unreasonable, however, to delve into how a brief half-hour's research trawling the web might enrich kids' experiences of lessons.

Visual Art as Stimulus

You can achieve an awesome amount of learning with the aid of twenty minutes on Wikipedia. I have zero learning about visual art. This, with the aid of the web, is easily remedied. Twenty minutes and you can acquire a veneer of learning that might, when combined with blather, be enough to convince a particularly gullible art historian of your learnedness. Here are lesson ideas taken entirely from a twenty-minute scan of Wikipedia's entries relating to American artists who were born between 1900 and 1920, few of whom I've ever heard of.

Edward Hopper's paintings are all redolent of back story. Visit *Road in Main* (1904) as stimulus for a written guided visualisation exercise; look at *Nighthawks* (1942) or *Room in New York* (1932) to examine relationships through

---

[20] David Byrne, Interview with *Source Magazine* at www.source.ie/issues/issues0120/issue17/is17artparhap.html

drama, or as the basis of a study of how body language gives us away; *New York Restaurant* (1922) or *Chop Suey* (1929) might be used as stimulus for writing an imaginative script which had an exploratory look at dialogue.

We write along to classical music – you don't? You should – it's fun. So why not write along to eye music? What work might we get out of the Rothko PowerPoint disco? Can we dance kinetic sculpture (à la the work of George Rickey)? Would teaching kids to be political cartoonists for a period every week benefit democracy? Would making approximations of Alex Liberman's painted steel structures in paper and card teach us anything about science? Can we better extrapolate mathematical learning from the work of geometric abstractionist Ilya Bolotowsky's work or from the cubists? Wouldn't it make sense to teach sociology through a study of pottery? Do a Google image search on these names. See what fires.

Visual Art as Recording Method

Here is where it gets interesting – if you were to draw all the major British newspapers in animal form, what would you come up with? *The Sun* as a many dugged pig, perhaps? *The Guardian* as a lion, *The Independent* as a turkey, *The Telegraph* as a dodo and *The Daily Mail* as a snarling pit bull? This is exactly how one *Times* cartoonist recorded them.

You can record sophisticated symbolic thought through cartoon. If we want to express fine distinction we can do so with a writing implement that is doing something other than writing. It does not always have to be an essay or a set of dully crass comprehension questions.

Every second-year English teacher is doomed to weary cognisance of the storyboarding activity that allows kids to spend time diluting language into a form which also incorporates drawing and colouring in. They are pleasing items for display; kids learn nothing at all from doing them, but it shuts them up for a while. Would they learn more if they were required to produce a complete comic themselves and had to command and manipulate a full sixteen or thirty-two page narrative? Would the study of comic art and convention that they would have to under-take in order to do so both engage and teach?

Why do all murals have to look like they were conceived of and drawn by the village idiot? Why aren't they in the style of Grayson Perry pots? Should we be making pots featuring narratives about kids' family histories painted on them?

Digital photography is increasingly being used as a means of recording. Curricularly [sic] appropriate versions of Damien Hirst's medicine cabinets (which were heavily influenced by Joseph Cornell's assemblages – check him out) would summarily answer the question, 'Why have you no artefacts in your display work?'

Could you teach kids to record their thoughts in the form of a linocut? Could we learn anything from the work of Frans Masereel, whose book, *Die Idee* (The Idea), tells two long-scale stories entirely in linocuts?

In 1912 Wassily Kandinsky produced a series of improvised woodcuts, and then wrote a piece of poetry about each one, collecting them together under a felt cover and calling the product Klange. Of it he said, 'I had the idea of a synthetic book that removed half of the old, narrow conceptions, breaking down the walls between arts.' It is a more ambitious objective for a scheme of work in primary than examining mini-beasts, but it is easily as achievable as that, and is a vastly more exciting idea. Everything is achievable. A teacher is only ever truly limited by the scope of their ambition.

Rock and Roll

The spoken form is in fact a very restrained representation of what is possible in the musical language.[21]

Robert Fripp

You might argue, and some do, that just as speech is simply movement suppressed, it is also a diluted form of singing.

Disc one of *Songs in the Key of Life* by Stevie Wonder taps me directly into a kaleidoscopic landscape of image. 'Village Ghetto Land' reminds me of English lessons at Kelsey Park School thirty years ago; 'Sir Duke' of a Dansette stuck on a cheap sideboard in a minuscule middle room in Penge, eighties MFI furniture, the beige shag-pile; 'I Wish' of my dear friend Resh Ariel's angular fluidity as a bass player as he inflicted his exquisite, sonic rootsiness and artisan's finesse on the blithe population of Maldon on an enchanting summer's day in the park. It was a lovely afternoon. I picture it.

Music attaches itself to image. Image is the brain's key means of storing memory. Why it is not being played all the time in every lesson in every classroom in every school in the land escapes me. I visit a lot of schools and, with the odd exception of the school steel band plonking away, I never really hear music in classes. Outside of the earlier years it appears that learning through song is

---

[21] Robert Fripp, Interview with *Axiom of Choice* at http://people.cs.uu.nl/jur/interviews/fripp.100299.html

anathema to most teachers. Whether this is as a result of kids having their sense of their own cool being violated if they are forced to sing, or of the teachers' irrational fear of their own tunelessness, I am not sure, but a teacher who was more interested in the learning of their charges than in what they looked like would jump headlong into the warm, watery arms of song and never look back.

A way of transitioning into song without that awful pregnant moment of silence where kids think en masse, 'By God. She wants us to sing. What shall we do? What shall we ever do?' is to sing with the hands first.

An example. Make up a lyric about the thing you want to teach. Here is a more than hastily cobbled together lyric of a song that, with substantial development, might be about how to use adverbs (with apologies to the Fun Boy Three). (And, although it sets a precedent, as I prefer never to apologise to these ladies in public, to Bananarama too.)

It's not what you're doing,
it's the way that you're doing it.

It's not that you're screwing,
it's the way that you're screwing it.

It's not what you're chewing,
it's the way that you're chewing it.

It's not what you're doing,
it's the way that you're doing it.

And that's what adverbs are.

The tune I am referencing here is (if you are senescent enough to recall it) both repetitious and monotonous. It was a hit.

You teach the tune first with finger clicks. There are four beats per line. The key is in making the finger clicking exercise fun to do for the (especially primary age) pupils. We reduce the lyrics to guttural grunts:

Uh-uh uh-uh-uh, uh-uh-uh uh-uh-uh-uh-uh.

But accompany these grunts with the four clicks per line, using both hands to click with and choosing a different spatial level for each line. We might start with our hands out slightly below the shoulders for the first line, then put them down towards the ankles for the second, above our heads for the third and back to just below shoulder level for the final line of the chorus. Doing this we teach the spindly tune first. Kids engage. We are just doing something daft.

There is no meaning to it. No learning. It is just a piece of fun. Then we introduce the lyrics. The kids engage with the lyrics because they are still enjoying the physicality of clicking their fingers and changing their positions as they do so. They learn the song and sing it with gusto. It sticks in their heads. Come exam time, if they want to recall the information contained in the song's lyrics, they merely recall the tune; the words come back easily as they are indelibly linked to an easily recalled melody.

Try this. It works.

There is a bald man who shares the surname Eno with a brand of liver salts and has the unpromising first name of Brian. He is a musician. But he does not play any musical instrument; neither is he a singer of any note or accomplishment. He was once in the pop group Roxy Music, in which he wore feathered, spangly, purple cat-suits and sat behind a synthesiser pressing the occasional button, wobbling the odd joystick. After leaving Roxy Music, he invented the concept of ambient music. One might argue that ambient music always existed, but he gave it a name, coming up with a series of albums called *Music for Lifts*, which seem to serve quite nicely as confirmation of Eno's claim that, 'Avant-garde music is sort of research music. You're glad someone's done it but you don't necessarily want to listen to it.' He has long since enjoyed the status of public intellectual.

Along with a friend of his, a painter called Peter Schmidt, he also devised a system of putting the plunger to artistic obstruction, calling this technique 'Oblique Strategy cards'. The idea was simple, though, of course, oblique ...

Imagine being in a recording studio. You are stuck. You scratch your head. What to do now? You pull out an Oblique Strategy card, which says something suitably vaporous like: 'Remove specifics and convert to ambigui-ties', 'Are there sections? Consider transitions', or 'Do nothing for as long as possible'. So far, so pretentious you might think. But I have worked with someone famous who has used them while making a record, and who swears so heartily by their powers for unlocking creativity that I wondered whether they might be of use in teaching.

Here are Eno's thoughts on the strategy cards as expressed in January 1980 to Charles Amirkhanian, a DJ on a US radio station called KPFA-FM Berkeley:

The Oblique Strategies evolved from me being in a number of working situations when the panic of the situation – particularly in studios – tended to make me quickly forget that there were other ways of working and that there were tangential ways of attacking problems that were in many senses more interesting than the direct head-on approach. If you're in a panic, you tend to take the head-on approach because it seems to be the one that's going to yield the best results. Of course, that often isn't the case – it's just the most obvious and – apparently – reliable method. The function of the Oblique Strategies was, initially, to serve as a series of prompts which said, 'Don't forget that you could adopt "this" attitude,' or 'Don't forget you could adopt "that" attitude.'[22]

As a principle, Eno's assertion that 'there (are) tangential ways of attacking problems that (are) in many senses more interesting that the direct head-on approach' rings true. The head-on approach doesn't always (or ever) produce the best results. You could adopt another, more oblique, approach to creativity.

It may be worth trying out the Oblique Strategies for yourself. They can be purchased at http://www.enoshop. co.uk for £30. I have done so. And the 'Do nothing for

---

[22] Brian Eno, interview with Charles Amirkhanian, KPFA-FM Berkeley, 1 February 1980.

as long as possible' card produces interesting results (though not, perhaps, of the kind you might want). It is an interesting exercise to use them, but as they are designed to relate specifically to the process of making either a record or painting, locating the possible link between the strategy and the classroom can be a little too oblique. Besides, both the 'Be dirty' and 'Tidy up' strategies are a little too much to bear. For antithetical reasons.

More useful is to create your own strategy cards that are specifically orientated around teaching.

Here are some (these are at the rear of the book in the Resources section ready to be cut up):

Try a completely different approach to discipline for ten minutes during the lesson. If you are relaxed, get hard; if you are hard, relax. Be explicit about it at the end of the ten minutes. Discuss the change of approach with your pupils and see if you learn anything.

What has this got to do with religion?

Perform a five-minute written activity where they have to use the hand they don't normally write with and have to speak about something else at the same time.

Get them writing a joke about the subject in pairs. Tell these at the end and judge whose is the funniest.

Use a carrot, tin opener or other readily available object to create an analogy that explains the learning.

Get them to copy off the board, but ... they must invent a rationale first and write a key with which they are going to represent the information in different colours and different sizes, upper case and underlined.

Ask them to draw what they know about a subject. Then cut the drawing into pieces, put them in some form of order and use the pieces of the picture as a prop with which to structure a presentation.

Ask them to sort the information into sets and present these as a Venn diagram.

Ask them to swap chairs with someone they haven't spoken to that week.

Ask them to doodle the learning for five minutes at the end.

Close your eyes. Visualise the future. Write about it.

A seven-part
lesson plan:

1. Draw it

2. Calculate it

3. Sing about it

4. Read it

5. Act it out

6. Think about it

7. Talk about it.

A grouped brainstorm for thirty minutes. Then get the groups to cross out any ideas they have ever heard of before. Collect all the ideas left in the class and display these as evidence of the class's originality and creativity.

Grouped discussion. How could they make money out of this information?

Discuss how you might find a way of colouring in that is properly cognitive.

Ask the lowest attaining child in the class to present at the end of the lesson. Be descriptive in your praise and then get the whole class to applaud them.

Get them to do a paired Mindmap® as the main lesson activity. Then take these away and ask each pair to tell another three pairs what was on their Mindmap®.

Draw a huge multicoloured picture of a fairy castle on the whiteboard to start the lesson.	Take a risk.
	Create an acronym. Learn it by rote.

When I am delivering a full day's INSET at a school, I ask every member of the school staff to come up with their four most left-field ideas about what they might do in a lesson and to write these down on a piece of paper. We collect these in a box; the idea being that there is a record of the staff's most creative ideas that may somehow be used as a resource. My favourite of these was from a well-attired art teacher – who may well be the only man I've ever met who has greeted middle age and found it didn't convert flamboyance into eccentricity – from Oasis Academy: Bristol who simply wrote the phrase, 'Abstract farmyard expression', on a piece of paper and retired from the exercise, rightly happy with his contribution.

As an example of what might be achieved if you collected all the most outré ideas of every member of staff in your school, here are the thoughts of the staff of Robert Napier School in Gillingham (2008–9). Read 'em, disagree with 'em, collect the most outrageous ideas of staff at your own school, make a wall display of them or, alternatively, print them on card (available in the Resources section at the rear of the book) and give them in a presentation box to every teacher, so that they might have them on their desk.

Pile up all the tables and use the floor space to create enormous paintings and drawings.	Choose a topic and create a poem by each pupil thinking of a line and putting them into some sort of order.
Plenary: ask the group to sum up everything they have learnt that lesson as a jingle.	Join in the activities with the students and present your work at the end.
Stand at the back of the room all lesson.	The cross-curricular conga.
Break the monotony of desk-based sessions. Five-minute task alternated with a run around the field. Continue until the end of the lesson.	Write their own sentences to describe probability words, cutting them out and sticking them on an appropriate label on the wall.

Sing the objectives.	Eat the lesson.
Draw a picture to illustrate a maths word. They are not allowed to label it.	Find a way of them swapping their bags being incorporated into learning.
Write the answers on the board. What's the question?	Turn classroom into a scene from a book, or battle, or country.
Pluck a hair off your head and describe it using only sound.	Paint a mural of the text being studied as a class.
Capital letter musical chairs.	Teach it with sign language.
Make finger puppets.	Produce a recipe for it.
Act out scenes from famous paintings.	Conjugate 'Amazing Grace'.

Tailor the whole lesson to music:

Starter music

Working music

Praise music

Assessment music

Plenary music

Cleaning away music

Pictionary.

Top Trumps® – collect together pictures of key figures in the subject (e.g. for PE, Pierre de Coubertin, Jesse Owens, etc.) and make into playing cards with different ability levels:

deviance – 80

sportsmanship – 10

power – 78

reputation – 90

Biology –
have the whole class act out cell plants.

Ask them why you chose that learning objective.

French – go outside and play boules to learn colours and prepositions.

Go into the playground and act out the alliances of the First World War.

Run around the field in bare feet shouting.

Dance the causes of the First World War.

Go around the school and measure angles. Look at all the shapes around the school and see how they are used.

Have them invent a machine to carry out a task and build it, e.g. a banana split making machine.

In teams, students use their bodies as the X and O, and play noughts and crosses, but no one can talk. Play for points, and if they talk the other team gets a point.

Idea relay: on Post-its® pupils put a question and answer, and they have to get all the pupils in their team (via relay) to know the answers.

Cooking with fractions.

Blindfold the pupils. They must feel an object or face. Take the object away. They must draw it without ever having seen it.

Paint with sticks.

Body painting. Go printing themselves onto large paper.

Washing-up liquid to demonstrate friction in science.

Teach an observed lesson without obeying any imposed rules.	Use digital cameras to represent what they have learnt in a photo.
Make a play about a scientific discovery, e.g. how the smallpox vaccine came about.	Take the students out of the classroom. Refuse to justify it to anyone who asks!

Would having these on a box in your classroom, ignoring the concept of planning and just obeying the cards, lead you to be a more or less interesting teacher for a week? Or would your head of faculty mouth the awful phrase, 'What would Ofsted say?'

I have heard this all too fearful utterance too many times: 'What about the National Curriculum?' There is a secret to dealing with these bodies and documents: ignore them. Who cares what Ofsted thinks? It is long about time that we, as a profession, stopped being concerned with the whimsical judgements of functionaries who may plausibly have been pretty rotten in the classroom themselves, and started being dictated to, instead, by our own professional fascination and creativity.

Ofsted, a regulatory body which should merely be checking and reporting, confuse their own role and feel they should be setting the agenda as to what is, or is not, 'good', 'satisfactory' or 'outstanding' teaching. They define this in a pitifully reductive way. A genuinely outstanding teacher will be sufficiently confident in their own abilities to not bother engaging in any real way with the central-ised attempt to define what it is they should be doing. Just be brilliant and they will forgive you for it. And if they don't, so what?

Let's replay this situation in another realm. Imagine any other art form where the critics, rather than simply report on what is happening in the field, actually set and publish the criteria for which a good review would be granted. It would rightly be perceived as madness. The idea of Rudolf Nureyev, Lawrence Olivier, Salvador Dali, David Bowie or Sir Stanley Bowles checking a set of rules pub-lished by a commentator to ensure they are complying with the accepted order of the form in which they work is risible. Yet it is a laughable idea to which educators accede, all too meekly. You will become what you could be through breaking all of those rules. Do the same as these artists. Ignore the critics' view of what is good and what is bad. It will make your work of more interest and value. The best judge of your work should be you, and seeking the views of outsiders to qualify it will only water down your vision.

Aside from Eno, there are practitioners in the realm of music whose opinions on creativity are of worth to the interested educator. Here are a series of songwriting tips from a guy called Antony Hegarty:

How to make the kind of music you want? Lie in your room and just make every single noise or bloodcurdling scream or moan of sound you ever wanted. Write down your dreams

every morning. If you can't remember them, write a dream
you wish you had. Imagine you carry ghosts inside you, and
write something down from one of their perspectives. Think of
a person who has hurt you, and sing for them. Think of
someone or something you have hurt, and imagine them
walking through a dream you have made for them.[23]

Imagine having him as your English or music teacher.
Imagine him planning your lesson. Imagine a dream in
movie form that has been forgotten for six months. Try
and remember it as the ghost. Use this as the starting
point from which to plan your lesson.[24]

Eno, when defining the process of creativity, suggests that
you should attempt to 'set up a situation that presents
you with something slightly beyond your reach'. It is just
such a process that can be used to explain why this book
does or doesn't quite work. I didn't know what I was
doing when I started writing it and know even less what
I am doing now it is nearing an end. His former band-

---

[23] Antony Hegarty, interview in *Word* magazine, June 2007, p. 27.

[24] **Starter**: Sit individually. Remember a dream from six months
ago. Get into pairs and tell your partner about the dream.
Guided: Teacher talk about the different conventions of writing
a first or a third person narrative. Why is it unlikely you will
ever read a second person narrative? (Because you, the reader,
are the main character.) **Independent**: Write down the details
briefly in sketch form. Now, rewrite it, changing the narrator
from being you to it being a ghost. Put in the ghost's thoughts
as to the nature of the dream. Put it into storyboard form.
Colour it in. Film it. **Plenary**: Did we learn more about narrative
device than we would have done with a comprehension
worksheet? (Rhetorical.) Do rhetorical questions have question
marks? (Rhetorical.)

mate, Bryan Ferry, once said, 'It's nice to know that there are several different avenues I could pursue.' I still have no idea how this book will end. It could go one of several ways. It might end with a fairy story ...

Which is by way of a cheap link into a long-standing and unfathomable obsession of mine with Bryan Ferry's peculiarly idiosyncratic style of (I think they call it) dancing. If you have not been gifted the chance to witness his bizarrely constipated, side-together-side-together-side conga it is readily available on YouTube, and I particularly recommend his performance of 'Jealous Guy' at Live Aid. His dancing here creates a whole new universe which exists far beyond the realm of poor. This pitiful obsession has infiltrated many areas. Whole Sundays have been wasted laying these on to the uncomprehending, living-room floor:

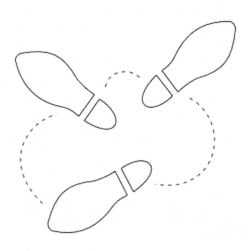

And I've waltzed drunkenly along to the dated strains of 'Avalon' in the style of Ferry, while my children look on, faces blanched in bemused horror. This obsession, which I believe is now entering the realms of the clinically unwell, has led to a further, perhaps even more pitiable, quest. To get these into lessons.

I have hundreds of them printed out, gathering dust, waiting (seemingly forever) for inspiration to strike. I am determined that one day they will feature in a lesson, and furthermore that the lesson will be the full consummation of a twenty-year obsession. It will charm and it will excite. It will produce rafts of learning that sail in on gales of laughter. Inspiration, however, steadfastly refuses to strike.[25]

---

[25] Should an idea of how one might use them to teach anything in English strikes someone, I would be grateful if you inform me immediately and rid me of a damaging obsession.

Words as Illustrators
of Concept

On the radio recently a man identified himself (proudly(!)) as having read the whole of the dictionary from cover to cover, going on to complain that it was a little scant on plot.[26] Little did the feller realise he was reading a series of many, many thousands of very short stories. A single word has (or should have to an interested mind) a potential infinity of resonances.

Try the following technique before planning an observed lesson. Clear an hour to indulge your creativity and sit with a blank piece of paper and a book. Any book. Turn to a page. Any page. Try page 16. Write down every sixteenth word you encounter in that book. Record the first twenty.

I took twenty from chapter 6 of *Chatterton* by Peter Ackroyd, a book I have never read, but have to hand for no explicable reason. Discard the rubbish and we are left with: goose-quill, deeds, is/was, one, I, Androcephalogoi, why, writ, singing, street and discordant.

Compare the words you have discovered to the subject you are about to teach. Use them as a structure. Like so.

---

[26] Incidentally, despite the fact that Peter Roget got his thesaurus together in 1805, it wasn't published till 1852. Forty-seven years touting his idea around the publishing houses: 'Well it's good Pete, but the story's not quite there yet.'

Subject

The possessive apostrophe (impossible to teach).

Starter

Provide children with feathers, knife, paper and ink. Ask who owns them? Model on the board the apostrophe in goose's quill. Ask children to carve a pen nib out of the feather and to write the phrase goose's quill on the paper provided.

Guided

Is/was – is there a difference between present and past tense in usage of the possessive apostrophe? 1. How to cope with possessive apostrophes and pluralisation. 2. What is your opinion of the apostrophe?

Independent

Write the diary of a man whose head is not far enough above his neck to be able to see if anyone is using possessive apostrophes.

Plenary

Why did they come about? Bring in a lawyer's writ and ask them to circle any possessive apostrophes. What do they notice about the rules of pluralisation?

As an alternative, we might take a biblical slant and plan a lesson on preposition usage with reference to every sixth word from chapter 20 of the Book of Revelation: come, key, dragon, shut, seal, deceive, loosed, saw, mark, reigned, lived, ears.

Map these at random against an alphabetised list of prepositions (see Resources section at the rear of the book).

Sixth word from Revelation 20	Alphabetised prepositions
Come	About
Key	Above
Dragon	Across
Shut	After
Seal	Against
Deceive	Along
Loosed	Amid
Saw	Among
Mark	Anti
Reigned	Around
Lived	As
Ears	At

It could be stimulus material for a creative piece. Alternatively, we might use it as a structure for a game of speaking and listening tag: separate kids into two teams, sit them opposite each other, give one side the list of words from the Book of Revelation, the other the prepositions. Ask them to create a story one line at a time using one of the words they have been given in each sentence. What do we learn about prepositions? Something (probably). I don't know what the outcome is yet. It hasn't been defined.

In pairs, kids could create a series of sentences featuring the revelatory words and with the alphabetised prepositions at the end of a sentence. They must then reorder the sentences so that the prepositions sit elsewhere. Could we boil down the words we have got from the Bible so we are left only with the nouns and draw pictures of these, then place these pictures in positions dictated to by the prepositions?

Speaking in Number

Can you measure a poem?

Can you calculate one?

You can certainly plot a graph of one.

A couplet is two lines; a quatrain is four. There are twelve couplet stanzas in the poem 'Limbo' by Edward Kamau Brathwaite. The graph below and table overleaf show the relationship between the number of words in the first and second line of each couplet.

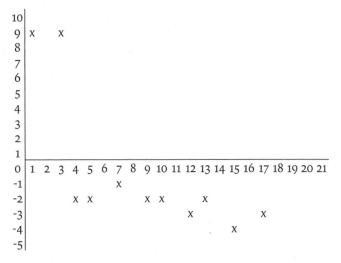

(X axis) Stanza number
(Y axis) Difference between the number of words in the first and second lines of couplet stanzas in 'Limbo'

Stanza number	A Number of words in first line	B Number of words in second line	Calculate the difference as the sum A − B =
1.	10	1	9
3.	10	1	9
4.	3	5	-2
5.	3	5	-2
7.	8	9	-1
9.	4	6	-2
10.	4	6	-2
12.	3	6	-3
13.	3	5	-2
15.	3	7	-4
17.	3	6	-3
19.	4	6	-2

The poem is about slaves' journeys, shackled together in appalling conditions below deck on a disease-ridden, effluent-strewn slave ship. What do you notice about the pattern created when we look at the numbers? Is it an accident?

Is anything a poet does an accident?

The two main core subjects are languages that never speak to each other. The teacher of mathematics respects the importance of the teacher of English's job, but distrusts the impurity of the language they specialise in, cannot understand their clothes and finds them garrulous socially. The teacher of English respects the importance of the teacher of mathematics' job too, but is acutely aware of the fact that of all subjects on the curriculum only his is capitalised (all subjects are equal, but some ...). But cannot bring himself to care so little about his appearance as to don the clothes the maths teacher wears without question. He also finds the mathematician a tad gauche socially.

And yet ... Perhaps their language is not as divorced as they thought. Or if it is, maybe it should be seeking a reconciliation.

A maths teacher at an independent school whom I met recently, a Mr Henry Bonnar, showed me a series of poems his students had written to a formula from the Fibonacci sequence.

Black	1 syllable
And	1 syllable
White are	2 syllables
All we see	3 syllables
Till we discover	5 syllables
Statistical uncertainty.	8 syllables

What other sequences might successfully be put in poetic form? Could we write binary poems? Tom Leonard, whose firebrand Glaswegian rants continue a brave, principled attempt to torch the smug edifice of our society's swaggering (C)onservative orthodoxy, created a form he called 'poster poems'. There is a derivation of these that produces interesting results and, again, is an accident of an approach that focuses on process. Ask students seven questions.[27] Then get them to edit their responses to a

---

[27] The seven questions and attached answers (which were loosely based around multiple intelligences) that gave rise to my poster poem were: 1. What is your favourite word? My father loves the word specific. I have no real favourites though I have always struggled with insignificance. 2. What is your favourite image? That of my wife holding someone else's child: she looked like

certain, limited amount of words for each answer and each line.

Specific insignificance	Line 1 – two words
Someone else's child	Line 2 – three words
Handsome	Line 3 – one word
Autistic	Line 4 – one word
Mother probably	Line 5 – two words
Worthy recipient of compassion	Line 6 – four words
Both and	Line 7 – two words

Whilst this is not a great example of the form, in the hands of children this technique really starts to swing. They can come up with a condensed version of language that can be strong enough to burn the palate; and they look great as display items when written in board marker on a large piece of sugar paper.

---

the Madonna. 3. What is your favourite song? I pretend that it is 'Holocaust' by Alex Chilton, but in truth it is 'Eight Stone, Tall and Handsome' by Avalanche. 4. Maths is boring. Discuss. I can find some autistic joy in the manipulation of number. 5. What does God look like? Someone's mother. Probably mine. 6. What do you think of yourself? Compassion comes easily to those who regard themselves as worthy recipients of the same. 7. Other people are? Both heaven and hell.

There is no reason whatsoever that the formula for the number of words per line could not be taken from a mathematical sequence.

Relatively recent developments in ICT have meant that we can take a piece of writing and reduce it to its numbers. The maths of a poem, for instance, can tell us a great deal about the writer's technique. Ratio of nouns to verbs: what does this tell us? A table of punctuation use: what does this tell us? Most repeated words: it will be obvious what this tells us, but until we did the maths, we might not have noticed or considered the obvious.

I Dreamed the Perfect Song

The singer, Bill Callahan, known generally (but by few people) as the one-man band, Smog, released a song in 2009 by the name of 'Eid Ma Clack Shaw'.[28] It is a lacerating take on the blanched emotional state people might find themselves in following the death of an important romantic relationship. In it, the narrator retires to the release of sleep to be haunted by dreams. 'I dreamed it was a dream that you were gone.' He then goes on to dream what he describes as 'the perfect song'. So good was it that he describes it as having, 'All the answers. Like hands laid on.' He scribbles it down. Waking in the morning to read the lyrics to that perfect song which contained all the answers, the lyrics read:

Eid ma clack shaw

Zupoven del ba

Mertepy ven seinur

Corfally ragdaur.

Which initially appear meaningless. Until you study them and read them back to front.

When they are confirmed as gibberish.

To me, though, it illustrates a certain part of the path to coming up with great ideas: the moment the idea appears, as if from nowhere, as if from a dream. Einstein

---

[28] If you wish to search this out, it is on an album called *Sometimes I Wish We Were an Eagle* by Bill Callahan.

(who regarded imagination as vastly more important than knowledge) suggested that you could invite these moments to appear more readily through a process of 'letting go, instead of looking for'.

And it is certainly possible to build a process of thinking that lays fertile ground for these moments. Webb Young, who we met in the first chapter, defines the stages of producing an idea:

1. Gather raw material. Google has made this grazing easy to do. When researching I tend to limit myself to the first two pages that Google throws up. Importantly, the first two pages of images too, as these can throw a whole new light on things, as well as giving material for the dreaded PowerPoint. Always throw in a wild card of the fifty-seventh (or so) page of results.

2. Then go away and digest the information. Take a walk. Come back to it when you feel ready.

3. Look at it from an entirely different angle. Record partial ideas. Riff. Travel up blind alleys.

4. Think about something else. Lie fallow. Let your unconscious do the work. Dream the solution. Cleanse your creative palate. Listen to some very loud music. Play the drums along with it. Involve yourself deeply in something that stimulates you but bears no relation to the task. Rest.

5. The idea appears. You dream the perfect song.

6. Reconcile yourself to failure and stop being a perfectionist. Good enough will do. Find it spindly. Accept it as so. Carve it so that it is good enough.

7. Serve it up.

Of course, once you have served it up, you may find that it was all complete rubbish. No matter.

Rip it up.

And start again.

Cut Up and Copy
Resources

English – Reading	Snooker
English – Writing	Darts
English – S and L	Football
Maths	Netball
Statistics	Hockey
Physics	Rugby
Chemistry	Cricket
Biology	Sprinting
RE	Egg and Spoon

List of subject areas and a further list of sports taken from pages 24–25

Geography	Hurdling
History	Wrestling
Sociology	Boxing
French	Tennis
ICT	Golf
Technology	Cycling
Citizenship	Disability Sport
PSHE	Swimming

Try a completely different approach to discipline for ten minutes during the lesson. If you are relaxed, get hard; if you are hard, relax. Be explicit about it at the end of the ten minutes. Discuss the change of approach with your pupils and see if you learn anything.

What has this got to do with religion?

Perform a five-minute written activity where they have to use the hand they don't normally write with and have to speak about something else at the same time.

Get them writing a joke about the subject in pairs. Tell these at the end and judge whose is the funniest.

Use a carrot, tin opener or other readily available object to create an analogy that explains the learning.

Get them to copy off the board, but ... they must invent a rationale first and write a key with which they are going to represent the information in different colours and different sizes, upper case and underlined.

Ask them to draw what they know about a subject. Then cut the drawing into pieces, put them in some form of order and use the pieces of the picture as a prop with which to structure a presentation.

Ask them to sort the information into sets and present these as a Venn diagram.

Ask them to swap chairs with someone they haven't spoken to that week.

A seven-part
lesson plan:
1. Draw it
2. Calculate it
3. Sing about it
4. Read it
5. Act it out
6. Think about it
7. Talk about it.

A grouped brainstorm
for thirty minutes. Then
get the groups to cross out
any ideas they have ever
heard of before. Collect all
the ideas left in the class
and display these as
evidence of the class's
originality and creativity.

Ask them to doodle the
learning for five minutes at
the end.

Close your eyes. Visualise
the future. Write about it.

Grouped discussion. How
could they make money out
of this information?

Discuss how you might
find a way of colouring in
that is properly cognitive.

Ask the lowest attaining
child in the class to present
at the end of the lesson. Be
descriptive in your praise
and then get
the whole class to applaud
them.

Get them to do a paired
Mindmap® as the main
lesson activity. Then take
these away and ask each
pair to tell another three
pairs what was on their
Mindmap®.

Take a risk.

Draw a huge multicoloured
picture of a fairy castle on
the whiteboard to start the
lesson.

Create an acronym. Learn
it by rote.

Pile up all the tables and use the floor space to create enormous paintings and drawings.

Choose a topic and create a poem by each pupil thinking of a line and putting them into some sort of order.

Plenary:
ask the group to sum up everything they have learnt that lesson as a jingle.

Join in the activities with the students and present your work at the end.

Stand at the back of the room all lesson.

The cross-curricular conga.

Sing the objectives.

Eat the lesson.

Break the monotony of desk-based sessions. Five-minute task alternated with a run around the field. Continue until the end of the lesson.

Write their own sentences to describe probability words, cutting them out and sticking them on an appropriate label on the wall.

Draw a picture to illustrate a maths word. They are not allowed to label it.

Find a way of them swapping their bags being incorporated into learning.

Write the answers on the board. What's the question?	Turn classroom into a scene from a book, or battle, or country.
Pluck a hair off your head and describe it using only sound.	Paint a mural of the text being studied as a class.
Capital letter musical chairs.	Teach it with sign language.
Make finger puppets.	Produce a recipe for it.
Act out scenes from famous paintings.	Conjugate 'Amazing Grace'.
Tailor the whole lesson to music: Starter music Working music Praise music Assessment music Plenary music Cleaning away music	Top Trumps® – collect together pictures of key figures in the subject (e.g. for PE, Pierre de Coubertin, Jesse Owens, etc.) and make into playing cards with different ability levels: deviance – 80 sportsmanship – 10 power – 78 reputation – 90
Pictionary.	

Biology – have the whole class act out cell plants.	Ask them why you chose that learning objective.
French – go outside and play boules to learn colours and prepositions.	Go into the playground and act out the alliances of the First World War.
Go around the school and measure angles. Look at all the shapes around the school and see how they are used.	Have them invent a machine to carry out a task and build it, e.g. a banana split making machine.
In teams, students use their bodies as the X and O, and play noughts and crosses, but no one can talk. Play for points, and if they talk the other team gets a point.	Idea relay: on Post-its® pupils put a question and answer, and they have to get all the pupils in their team (via relay) to know the answers.
Cooking with fractions.

Paint with sticks. | Blindfold the pupils. They must feel an object or face. Take the object away. They must draw it without ever having seen it. |
| Run around the field in bare feet shouting. | Dance the causes of the First World War. |

Teach an observed lesson without obeying any imposed rules.

Use digital cameras to represent what they have learnt in a photo.

Body painting. Go printing themselves onto large paper.

Washing-up liquid to demonstrate friction in science.

Make a play about a scientific discovery, e.g. how the smallpox vaccine came about.

Take the students out of the classroom. Refuse to justify it to anyone who asks!

Come	About
Key	Above
Dragon	Across
Shut	After
Seal	Against
Deceive	Along
Loosed	Amid
Saw	Among
Mark	Anti

Every sixth word from chapter 20 of the Book of Revelation and random alphabetised list of prepositions, see page 73

Reigned	Around
Lived	As
Ears	At

More books by Phil Beadle

How To Teach ISBN: 9781845903930

Bad Education: The Guardian Columns
ISBN: 9781845906832

Altogether Now ... The Ultimate Plenary Book
ISBN: 9781781350539